GOD WILL LEAD THE WAY

Edited by

Jessica Woodbridge

First published in Great Britain in 2005 by
TRIUMPH HOUSE
Remus House,
Coltsfoot Drive,
Peterborough, PE2 9JX
Telephone (01733) 898102

All Rights Reserved

Copyright Contributors 2005

SB ISBN 1 84431 078 7

FOREWORD

In today's modern world everyone's life is fast-moving and hectic, leaving little time to stop, open our minds and gather together our thoughts. However, there are times when we really do need to take time out to sort our feelings and emotions. Poetry can very often provide us much-needed release by allowing us to express and share our important thoughts with others.

God Will Lead The Way is a special collection of these poems, featuring the work of new and established authors of today.

Together they combine their creative talents to present to you an inspiring and enjoyable read that you will want to return to time and time again.

Jessica Woodbridge
Editor

CONTENTS

THANK YOU

Thank You Father
For night and day
Thank You Father
You are there
As we pray,
Thank You Father
For the great love
That You showed us
From Your Son above,
We thank You
From Your throne on high,
Would hear us
When we pray or cry,
We thank You that
You came to Earth
To show us of
Eternal birth.

Lillian R Gelder

Untitled

I close my eyes
My Lord You seek
Seek to ease my troubled sleep
You hold my dreams, my hope, my fears
A comfort to ease my many tears
Guide me, sweet Lord towards the light
As this day turns into night

I close my eyes
A prayer I make
You take my hand to guide me straight
To love, to hope, my soul is true
The truest reflection I have found in You
Lord, the truth.

Sally Williams

Bedtime Prayer

Oh loving God, who from our enemies hath defended us
Oh loving God who clothes and shelters, feeds us
Through fire and shell and homeless hell
Your love our rock and shelter
Great praise we raise for all our days
Grateful for Your mercies

Oh generous God who give us love so special
Your trumpet sounds whilst faith abounds
And *love* holds all together
Cross stormy seas and matrimony
Keeps safe in any weather

And wondrous *hope* You give each one
A prize so great when race is run
That through Your Son, our Lord the Christ
You give us all eternal life

'And You will wipe away every tear and death will be no more'.

At quiet times we think of You and as crisis rages raise our pleas
But oh divine one You have us in mind all times no matter what
Let our thoughts be to praise Thee
Let our action do honour to Thee
Let our hearts strive to love Thee

We strive to walk in Thy path though oft times we stray
Yet Your divine light is there to guide us each and every step of the way
Let us march straight and true to the task that You set
Let us carry burdens willingly to the place that You set
Let us meet all objectives with relish You set!

'Surely Your goodness and mercy shall follow me all the days of my life'.

Barrie Webster

BEDTIME PRAYER

As I close my eyes to pray,
I thank You for another day,
For all Your love and constant care,
And Your guidance every day.
For all my friends and family,
Be they near or far away,
I remember them each day,
And for them I also pray,
Bless us now and always,
As we journey on life's way,
Guard and guide and keep us,
Each and every day.
Amen.

Esther Herron

SIMPLICITY

A simple prayer, to guide us off to sleep
To thank God for caring,
As we prepare to count our fluffy whitened sheep.
A simple plea, as under our duvets we respectfully creep.
Amen, as we look above, as we down -
Ourselves - peacefully off to sleep.

Elaine Hind

PRAYER FOR THE EVERYDAY PERSON

Dear Lord, protector of all our souls.
Forgive me if I stray too far from Your humble dwelling,
without Your blessing.

The stresses of daily life are all confusing, all consuming.
Give me strength to go *back to basics,*
to concentrate on what I know is Your word.

May You bless all those around me.
Those in pain, those in trouble, those who grieve.
Give them courage to face the challenges for the day ahead.

Help me be true to myself and my faith.
Don't let me be ashamed of what I know is Your love
and Your care.

Thank You, dear Lord for Your guidance,
set me on the right path in life
So that I may live to know You better.
Amen.

Anita Curnin

ANGELS

Not just beings with ethereal wings,
When my angel protects me, my heart smiles and sings.
There are good ones and bad ones, but the bad we'll ignore,
Besides in their powers we don't hold much store.

If you're feeling down or are suffering pain,
Ask for your angel, you've much you can gain.
You may not believe in them, not at the first,
But there's no harm in trying, if things can't get worse.

Your angel is there for you, you just have to ask.
You may not be able to complete a task
Without having aid from an unselfish power,
With a touch so delicate, just like a flower.

When an idea comes unbidden to you
It could be your angel right out of the blue,
Carrying messages, because that's their work,
Accept as a gift, a most welcome perk.

They may be invisible to you or I,
But there are some of us who are able to spy
A sign that their angel is hovering near.
They are the lucky ones, that much is clear.

But don't give up hope because vision is lacking,
An angel can work without visible backing.
You may feel their touch on the back of your hand,
And then recall that things work out unplanned.

At least you've not planned it the way it's worked out,
But life is a mystery, of that there's not doubt.
So be there for your angel as he's there for you
And pick up those messages right there on cue.

Christine Bridson-Jones

A Prayer Of Parting Thoughts

Be still
And know your nightmares are ours too a while
Until tomorrow's sun drives them away.

Be calm
And keep the memory of our memories of your smile:
No harm can come to you if that will stay.

Don't fret
That anything will change or disappear;
Forget the thought that you might be alone.

Don't fear
Those new horizons that will greet your eye and ear,
For here the ones who love you ever
Always are your own.

Richard Kitchen

Prayer For Victims Of Crime

It is written: *He heals the broken hearted*
And binds up their wounds. Psalm 147:3.

We can't imagine their fears
Their incessant tears,
The vulnerability, their humiliated side;
Of the lives that are shattered,
Lives that once mattered,
Left broken and empty inside.

We can't imagine the heartache
They may feel each new daybreak,
The torment that lasts through the day;
Nor imagine their plights,
The dark, sleepless nights,
For them, Lord, we pray.

Holy Spirit all revealing,
Lord, bring them healing,
From the nightmares, brokenness and pain;
Lord, heal their heartache,
That the sun rise one daybreak,
That their lives will matter again.
Through Jesus Christ. Amen.

Ray Varley

That I May Know You

My humble heart cleaves unto Your
Awesomeness
My passive soul rejoices over the wonders
Of Your hands
The sun bites us by day and later
Evanescence
The rain drops at night and later dies down
But in all these none answers,
None asks!
The waters of the sea dance to Your praises
The birds sing Your melody day long
Even the flowers smile all through with
Beauty in their eyes
Just as the heavens behold Your majesty
And my soul, oh my soul marvel at this dark hour
With one thirst
That I may know You . . .

Joseph Iregbu

GOD'S PLAN

What is it?
While Muslims pray five times a day
We pray when we can.

Divine providence
Is that God's plan?
Would it make sense?
If Christians prayed five times a day
And Muslims when they can.

Prayer and meditation
Are the keys to being man.
They unlock love and compassion
Make us all part of God's plan.

Is providence a lucky chance?
Can living be divine?
Can we make a better world
In our short lifetime?

Torah, Bible and Koran
Teach us a way of life
But to follow we would have to live
According to God's plan.

Maria Dabrowska

Spirit Guide

I enter my place,
Green shades and blue,
Hands start to tingle,
As I'm thinking of You,
Invaluable teachings,
You are always there,
To offer advice, guidance and care.
The spirit guide teaches.
With light and with love,
Divine inspiration,
Sent from above.

Simon McCreedy

UNTITLED

I snuggle up warm and curl up tight
Then I close my eyes so there is no light
I know as I lay fast asleep
Good fairies fly round, should I peep?
They fly and protect me while I dream
Nothing bad so I won't scream
God bless the fairies who keep me calm
I will make sure they come to no harm

Susan Brown

THE CANDLE IN OUR LIVES

The flickering light from a candle,
Transforms the dark of night,
By the touch of its wavering fingers,
Shines twinkling, yellow light.

The candle has a limited life,
According to its size,
And gives its all, when lit by us,
Constantly shining until it dies.

The analogy of the candle,
That gives the darkness light,
Can be compared with a special one,
Born the very first Christmas night.

His limited life in human form,
Was when He walked this Earth,
And brought new light to you and me,
Much more than we are worth.

Yet He gave His all, to save us,
Unworthy, though we be,
He is the light that lives in us,
Giving new life for you and me.

So let us thank our candle,
He's Jesus Christ the Lord,
For lighting up our darkened lives,
By being our Saviour, Light and Word.

Nigel Lloyd Maltby

My Saviour

If I stole from every poor man,
Just to feed my habits
If I slated Your name and denied Your love for me
Would You love me then?

If I lived it up with Satan,
Being selfish and full of sin
Came crawling back to You one day
Would You love me then?

If I lived to serve my own greed
And damaged this body You gave me, hating every inch
Would You love me then?

If I shut You out of my life
And wouldn't let You in
Would You love me then?

See, Lord I know You died for me
To take away my sin
So answer me this question
Would You love me then?

Now I know Lord
This heart of mine has been filled
With true love from You to me
For eternity I'm told

And now I realise
Yes, my God, my Saviour
And my best friend
You would still love me then.

Bethany Meakin

Nativity

Can you hear the bells are ringing?
It is to you they are calling
Come on come inside to see
The joy, of the nativity.

Listen the choir are singing
Peace on Earth He is bringing
In a stable cold and bare
Jesus came our lives to share.

Now as He lies quietly asleep
The shepherds come bringing a sheep
The angels told them of His birth
God's only Son born on Earth.

Then on that very night
Shone a star, new and bright
That star had planted a seed
So wise men followed its lead.

Bearing gifts they journeyed on
At the stable they found God's Son
Frankincense, myrrh and gold
Gifts for a King, a Lord.

So listen as the bells ring
Enter in with the choir, sing
For peace on Earth kneel and pray
The joy of Heaven is yours today.

Joan Williams

Abide With Thee

Take my hand. I feel so lonely.
Hold me close. Don't let me go.
Dry my tears. My heart is aching.
Broken dreams are all I know.
God is love, the Bible tells us.
Love divine is what I need.
When all earthly friends desert me,
Sweet Jesus I'll abide with Thee.

Rosemary Thomson

A GODLY WOMAN

A godly woman is full of joy.
She doesn't grumble over her work, the amount of washing up,
Or the number of double-glazing calls she gets in one afternoon.
A godly woman is full of peace.
She doesn't have to worry about where she's going when she dies,
Or have a panic attack every time her husband looks at a motorbike.
A godly woman is full of patience.
She doesn't mind waiting in a traffic jam, queuing in a shop,
Or waiting on the phone for hours whilst someone picks their teeth.
A godly woman is full of kindness.
She helps the aged, gives words of comfort to those that have fallen,
And doesn't scream at spiders and flush them down the toilet.
A godly woman is full of faithfulness.
She will stick close by a friend, who is going through a hard time,
And a husband who just knocked all the cut glass off a shop shelf.
A godly woman is full of gentleness.
She kisses away all the pains of a child, soothes a troubled mind,
And never hits, kicks or mauls the computer when it refuses to work.
A godly woman is full of self-control.
She is calm,
when her new white carpet is covered in red wine,
And never loses her head when dealing with deaf sales assistants.

I think I am a work in progress.

Ceri Siân

Fool's Circle

There have been times in my life
When I doubted or lost my faith
With the death of my wife
I lost all belief in life, in God, in me.

Yet every time I get lost
Every time I cry
A voice deep inside asks why!
I travel in circles
Back to my roots and faith.

I lost it first after my bar mitzvah
I couldn't see the point
With mates of all beliefs
What was mankind fighting for?

I found it in Germany
In a synagogue surrounded by a convent
I lost it when my parents died
And found it in an extermination camp
And in the eyes of Bosnian children
I lost it when my wife was taken from this mortal plane
My friends found it and returned it to me.
I will never lose it again.

Believe what you choose to believe, but believe in it totally
Never lose your faith, whatever that may be
Don't keep travelling at angles and tangents
Do not! Travel in the Fool's Circle like me.

Derek Blackburn

A Poem To The Inglorious Dead

There once was a day when murder was wrong,
When life was a gift and our morals strong,
And yet today we kill without thought,
Even argue the right for the choice to abort.

What of a child that should have been born?
Of their small, sacred soul left lying forlorn?
Of ten tiny fingers and ten tiny toes?
Of unborn eyes, ears, mouth and nose?

When is a life yours to take?
Murder is never a stupid mistake.
Aborting is killing a person within,
Oh when will we realise to kill is a sin?

Patricia Hazel Scurfield

THE POWER OF PRAYER

Lord, I know not the words of prayer,
Which were offered on my behalf,
From friend and stranger alike,
I too asked for Your intervention,
To change the outcome,
Of the serious diagnosis,
That the year 2004,
Had bestowed upon me.

I thank You for the power of prayer,
And the light,
With which You pierced the despair of my spirit,
When plunged into the darkest depths of the soul,
Faced with my mortality,
My faith was tested to the limits,
Yet I discovered,
That I am not alone here on Earth.

The threads of the divine,
Are just a prayer away,
Ask in faith and you will receive,
Flames of hope were sent forth in each candle lit,
Words offered were heard,
Giving me strength of body and spirit,
To face all placed before me,
My faith renewed in the face of adversity.

Ann G Wallace

Thank You, Lord

For the miracle of birth
For the beauty of the Earth,
The sheer joy of human love
For all blessings from above.

For the chance of doing good
To understand, be understood,
To help my needy fellow man
To make a difference where I can.

Thanks for giving up Your life
Entering this world of strife,
The hope for mankind to be free!
How disappointed You must be!

Thanks for the chance to try again
To ease our own and others' pain,
It's never pointless in the end
I'm counting on You as my friend!

I thank You Lord, for being there
For listening to my humble prayer,
For stretching out eternity
I know You will remember me!

Moira Wiggins

THE CROSS

What held You to the cross that Friday?
The nails weren't enough
The soldiers were too weak
There was nothing that could keep You there
Except You

You chose to stay
To suffer
Terribly
For me

You chose to stay
To endure the pain
To hear the mocking
To feel the abandonment
Because of Your love
For me

Your love was strong enough
To hold You on that cross
Stronger than the nails
More powerful than Roman forces
Even greater than the pain
Your love held You there
For me

Sarah Auld

BIRTH OF A SON

I saw a bright shining light
Hovering in the sky
'Twas o'er the town of Bethlehem
To show Jesus was nigh

And so became an era
For a fallen, sinful world
Of God's might, grace and power
His forgiveness thus unfurled.

O lovely town of Bethlehem
That sheltered God's own Son
Born as a babe on Christmas morn
The loving, holy one.

So lift your voice to praise Him
For all that He has done
To bring us to His Father
The gracious, merciful Son.

P J Laing

THE LORD IS MY HELPER

My help comes from the Lord
Who gives me strength
For each day.
Helping me to cope
With whatever comes my way.

Never alone
With Jesus by my side.
For He is always there
Ready to lend a helping hand.

He gives me hope,
Encouragement and help.
He sends people to my aid.
He sends me His love
His greatest gift
Because He loves me so.

Julie Smith

GOD'S LOVE IS LIKE . . .

God's love is like floating in Heaven.
God's love is like a gentle whisper that says love.
God's love is like a shining star in the night.
God's love is like hugging your friends.
God's love is like my friendship with Adrianne and Coral.
God's love is like when my mum and dad take me on holiday.

Laura Harper (9)

THE AMENDMENT

Time has evolved,
the hour is now,
and change it now is due,
and I must introduce,
a new vital law for you.

Thou shalt not violate a child,
nor cause them pain or ill,
nor bring them harm in any way,
this is your *Lord God's* will.

Silence your tongue
and still thy hand,
when angered, turn away,
my lambs must not be victimised,
in any kind of way.

Heed this my eleventh commandment
memorise it well
for those, who recognise it not
should fear my wrath, full well.

Jacqueline Claire Davies

EXPOSITION OF THE TURIN SHROUD

How calm those timeless eyes lie closed in death.
Is this the author of the starry sweep;
and dare we call such icy stillness sleep,
when that majestic face stirs not for breath.

What peace that mighty countenance reveals.
What agony the injured flesh defines.
Why lies the forehead free of anguished lines,
incongruous with the scourge's bloody weals.

Could thus the Crucified so gently rest,
his soul in conflict at the gates of Hell;
to break them down and shepherd out the swell
of captives, freed to dwell among the blest.

But of that fight his slumber does not show;
sound sleeper of the borrowed shroud and tomb.
The god-like image fixed upon the loom-
wove linen, holds no certainties to know.

My doubts would fly like Magdalene's that dawn,
should those deep eyes, when opened, gaze on me.
Sleep on and leave me in uncertainty:
I dread that you might be the virgin-born.

I could not then endure that holy face;
for in those eyes of God I would behold
the truth that he upon the mountain told
and know myself to be too far from grace.

And yet the simple fishermen withstood
that awful visage and did not despair.
What wells of mercy did they drink of there,
to make their insufficiency seem good.

Rod Munday

SEARCHING

The soul is strong, the body weak
Yet still we will continue to seek.

We want to know what lies ahead
What it's really like when we are dead.

They say that life is eternal, if we follow the light
But do they really know? Are they definitely right?

So many unanswered questions, the answers we must find
If we are to pass over with absolute peace of mind.

So we must follow Great Spirit, that unconditional love
To find truth and understanding, harmony, peace and love.

It is not always easy to follow in the way they say
Daily we find obstacles that push us hard to stray.

With absolute resolve, we must follow that Great Light
That we understand the truth and know that they are right.

Ann Elizabeth Bruce

The Hiding Place

Lord, it gets so lonely, here on my own,
Sometimes desperation fills my heart.
Life goes on apace around me,
But I don't feel a part.

It's easy then for self-pity to take me on a trip
Down memory lane - is this what You
Want me to see and hear? I start to dip
Into the past and find it's an abyss.

A big hole full of hurts and fears
Of lack of trust and love,
Of broken promises and dreams
That I can't rise above.

'Lord God, where are You now?'
I cry, despair in every bone.
'I'm here beside you and around you.
I love you still, my son.

I am a hiding place for you,
But you need to hide in Me,
To shut your ears and eyes and thoughts
And determine not to flee

To other forms of comfort,
But to find your rest in Me.
I am a hiding place for you
And here I'll always be.

So when the pain seems dark and drear
And pain is all you feel
Just run to Me, you need not fear
You know My love is real.'

Margaret Pagdin

CRYING OUT TO JESUS

When you are down
Reach up to the heavens
Call out to Jesus
He will listen and answer

Prayer can be like
An emergency 999
Phone call
Jesus may not answer
Physically but get
Ready for amazing
Dreams and pictures
And wound full words
Of wisdom
Or may be strong
Answer of prayer
Because Jesus is
Ready to help
So just ask Him
He will help

James Green

HEALING

Frozen flakes fall softly,
Kissing this car,
This face,
This skin.
Cradled in the cosy comfort
Of a caterpillar's cocoon.
We propel onwards
Cruising these crystal roads.

Pain melting like warm butter,
Trickling slowly away.
Light around me.
Light beneath me.
Light within me.
Darkness be damned.
Go back from when you came.

Blessed becomes too small a word
Beneath the bliss of these gentle brushes.
Eternal whispering
Words of wisdom.
Enwrapped in the familiar folds
Of an angel's wings.

Tracey Levy

Secured In Him (I Am)

Once I was lost and full of sin
I bent my knees and prayed to Him
My hands were clasped and full of sweat
Like an actor on his very first set
My heartbeat was fast like a lamb lost
To find its mother at all its cost
When Mother was found he was secure
Safe at her side and worried no more.
Back to my senses and fully calm
I felt the Lord Jesus holding my arm
'Be still,' He said, 'and be troubled no more
My Father in Heaven has sent me to cure
Your sins and sickness and soul He saves.'
'O Lord remember me in my last days
For eternity is only a heartbeat away.
When I wake up no price to pay
My Lord was pierced for all my sins
I'll fly in Heaven His praises to sing.'

W N Brown

My Prayer

Sitting on my bed at night ending my day with You,
It's time for our chat Lord and come close to You
Thank You for looking after me, my family and friends
And all the good work that You do.

Thank You for the wonderful world that we live in,
You're the cleverest person I know,
Looking down on us with angels at Your side,
O Lord You give me so much pride
I know You will always look after me
Be there when I need You most
Thank You for being such a good host.

If I can help someone in my day
I know that You made me in the right way,
To be helpful and kind, honest and true,
Why can't all people be like You?
I am getting tired now Lord and have to sleep,
I will keep You in my thoughts Lord
And close to my heart,
I will talk to You tomorrow when it gets dark.

Maddie Reade

Doctrine

Many laws of faith there be,
Across the lands, oceans and seas,
Some dictate others' lives,
If they should marry have children or wives,
Some guide us politely to spiritual calm,
Solitude, abstinence; others do harm,
Blood-letting rituals, done in the name of God,
Human sacrifice, gifts to Gog,
Nature flexes its muscles, sometimes takes souls,
When neglected it feels, then scores a home goal,
Tree hugging we do, to be at one,
Then decimate things that can't be undone,
Then with hands together, we pray, look aloft,
When pestilence and famine are the cost,
When all seems lost, we *trust in the Lord,*
Then slay one another, counting the score,
Excuses we use for our zealous ways,
Then chant doom, watching the days,
Religion is man, confusion and doubt,
Wanting meaning of life, when he has no clout,
Wrestling with thoughts, what's on the other side?
Prophets and charlatans only offer a guide,
Holding hands in a ring, we talk to the dead,
Listening to the past to what was said,
Usual rituals and magic, gold trinkets bright,
Moon phases some use to get an insight,
The Holy books teach us; in a cryptic message,
The value of life: it's a difficult passage.

Josh Brittain

IF ONLY

Wouldn't it be lovely if pets didn't die,
If flowers were forever and people could fly?

Wouldn't it be great if we could talk to the dead,
And if all politicians meant what they said?

Wouldn't it be fun if we didn't get old,
And knew about turning lead into gold?

Wouldn't it be nice if we didn't have to try
To find answers to questions beginning with 'why'?

Wouldn't it be good if the world was all clean,
And . . .

Wouldn't it be marvellous if *God* could be *seen?*

Jenny Fernandes

ODE TO THE HOLY ROSARY

In Joy, Light, Sorrow and Glory,
beads of love,
in prayer and meditation,
linking Earth to Heaven.
The saving help,
spread throughout the world.
The prayers of love -
to God and Our Lady,
the decades, linking -
forever, God and Our Lady;
from before the Conception
of Jesus,
to the Coronation
of His Mother, Mary.
Heaven's link
to Earth.
Roses in beads,
to help our world.
God and Mary,
linking hands with us.
Alleluia. Alleluia.

E B M M Wreede

The Ambulance Bus

'The wheels of the bus
go round and round'
as it bumps
along the ground
and the phrase resounds
in my head
as I head
for radiotherapy

'The wheels of the bus'
stop, another passenger
boards, politeness
of a morning greet
weak but made
nonetheless

'The wheels of the bus'
go round again,
four, five of us
making progress

'The wheels of the bus'
will stop their circling
one day soon
for us ending
treatment
it's tiring, writing,
radiotherapy makes me tired

'The wheels of the bus
go round and round'
thank you nursery rhyme
for seeing me through
for lightening my view
as I write with vigour anew
I wish passengers
after me, recovery
from a tiring time,
time circling less as God does bless.

P A Findlay

LEAD ME GENTLY INTO YOUR ARMS

'Lead me gently into Your arms' -
A voyage of self discovery,
taking me along the path of destiny,
leading to the river of life,
crossing over the bridge of sighs,
through the fields of dreams,
leading to the summit of the mountain of hope,
whilst encountering valleys of tears along the way,
until the *gate* appears at the beginning of the rainbow,
where I will find *You,*
the answer to my prayers,
in Your sacred domain -
by invitation only!

'Lead me gently into Your arms' -
Let me follow Your guiding light,
and hear Your 'still, small voice',
when reaching the many crossroads of life,
please give me the willpower to stay on course,
overcoming obstacles and temptations on the journey,
keeping always the final destination in my sights,
of a beautiful new world, with a new beginning,
with the *'Greatest Love of All'* -
patiently waiting for me,
with a heart that is overflowing with love,
and arms outstretched into eternity,
cradling me in an embrace, with a sweet fragrance
in the 'spirit' of everlasting love and peace,
where I can feel safe in Your arms for evermore!

'Lead me gently into Your arms'

Lisa S Marzi

HOME TO GOD

'You smiled in sleep,
Pain lines no longer keep
their place upon a smiling face -
Let me ease your pain away -
so that you smile again today.'

'In dreams I smiled . . .
I was again a child . . .
around me there was nought but love.
Stripped of the world's veneer
I knew no fear - a childhood God was near.
My soul, the unknown part of me,
my ticket to eternity, awoke and smiled.
We clung to love and would not let it go -
My soul and I.
This long last mile fast leads me
to the Heavenly Land - hold tight my hand!
Hear Heaven and Earth unite to sing
The angel chorus, 'Welcome Home'!
Laughter in Heaven, how it rings and wings
its way through all creation.
Today and every day we pray love brings
all oft forgiven sinners - home to *God.'*

Christina Crowe

God The Creator

God the creator King of my heart,
This day I will rejoice in all things,
All things formed here upon Earth,
And with a humble heart I shall sing.

The word was with God,
From the very beginning of time,
The might and power of the word,
Showing forth truth, touching the divine.

The word was in the world,
Given to those hearts who would receive,
God of hearts sent His Holy Spirit
To those poor and lost who would believe.

The world was sent a Saviour,
From the realms of peace above,
Came to teach the truth to give new life,
With His outstretched hands, words of love.

The Lamb of God for we shall praise You,
Alleluia we shall cry and sing,
For we have victory upon the cross,
Jesus of love of hearts so forgiving.

Such grace and wonder would follow,
The Son, who travelled far and wide,
Spreading the good news of the living God,
With the Holy Spirit by His side.

'Be still,' He said, 'it is I, Jesus,
For I have come to save the lost and the poor,
To give them light and to know new life,
A blessed peace in hearts for evermore.'

Simon Foderingham

Lady Mary

Lady of the loving heart
Whose Son saved all mankind
Lead us when we think of Thee
With hearts and thoughts and minds.

Lady, Mother of our Saviour dear
Whose Son was sinned against by man
Who gave us all our liberty
Through time's endless span.

Lady Mary lead us
Like children with faltering feet
Teach us how to follow Jesus
Seated peaceably around Your dainty feet.

Lady of the twilight years
Whose Son was torn and slain
Whose unhesitating humble heart
Guided the disciples when her Son was wrenched away.

Lady Mary hear us, when we pray.

Jane Dyson

Day By Day

Please *Lord* help me
Day by day,
To be a Christian
In *Your* way,
To do the things
You want me to,
To *love* my brother
As I love *You.*

Patricia Edwards

THE BIBLE POEM

With each page of this book I read,
May I give You more of me to lead.
And may each word here be a seed
That grows to fruit my soul to feed.

Let it plant in me a great desire,
A hunger for Your spirit's fire,
A longing that I might serve
At the feet of the One who deserves.

May its proverbs and instruction
Keep me from the Devil's destruction,
Help me to always remain pure
Through the trials and hardships that I shall endure.

And forever, through day and night,
I will always fight the good fight,
I will always do that which is right,
And I will everywhere shine Your light.

Jonathan Best

A Babe Born To Be A King

God bless this babe,
So meek and mild,
Keep a close watch
On this Heavenly child.

Keep Him safe
As He sleeps
His mother too,
As she keeps -
A gentle watch
On her son,
A special babe,
The Holy One.

Debbie Nobbs

TIME AND FAITH

In childhood I was cared for and loved,
Blissfully unaware that true blessings came from above,
The ups and downs of life I accepted as the norm,
Until the day a dark shadow enveloped our home.

My childhood had gone, of that I was sure,
A dilemma so final was painful to endure,
To be a grown-up at eleven, I did not know how,
So I struggled on in the shadows with no way out.

But life really does go on in a different way,
The joy and peace had gone out of every day,
Until the hope around the corner was a baby brother,
He needed us, we needed him, and we needed each other.

Our baby was baptised in the deepest, snowy winter,
At a church where I felt peace when I entered,
A chest infection in the baby caused a crisis one night,
In panic I ran outside into a dark porch with no light.

Only six months ago, Dad died under coal down the mine,
Reality and truth were bereft of time,
Now I had time to seek urgent help - but from where?
The doctor had done his best, I felt helpless and scared.

I dropped to my knees, tearfully humble to pray,
I prayed The Lord's Prayer with hands together a child's way,
Then I crept back indoors where Mum confided,
Like an answer to my prayer, the crisis had subsided.

Kathleen McBurney

JUDGEMENT DAY

It was another evil day on planet Earth,
With thickening smoke from the churches on fire,
People indulging in sinful mirth,
Under-age sex and babies for hire.

Then all of a sudden there was an angry blast,
The rain turned to blood and the winds got stronger,
Christians yelling, 'The Lord has come at last,'
The Devil's paradise will be no longer.

The sky was scarlet as the angels neared,
Towards us in graceful flight,
Above everyone's head a number appeared,
All coloured red, but some were white.

They lined us up and read the law,
There was a queue to Heaven and a queue to Hell,
They listed all our good deeds, and every flaw,
We marched in time to a calling bell.

Pulled along by his red-hot chain,
The men were stabbed, and the women stripped,
Liars, thieves, doctors insane,
My friends, my relatives, my destiny gripped.

From afar 'The Angel of Death' was calling,
Our wicked lives were always Hellbound,
They put bags over our heads to stop us bawling,
All we saw were the hoof prints on the ground.

We heard the wails and smelled the burning,
From the roaring pit of the damned,
And we knew that was it, there was no returning,
When the creaking, iron gates slammed.

It was the day of judgement, the day the world shook,
The day the Christians were received,
And all the black souls that the reaper took,
Are burning in Hell because they never believed.

Ian McNamara

Pride Goeth

When Cain presented an unfit gift,
he gave it only a cursory inspection,
his pride expecting a heavenly lift,
but instead he received only rejection.

When Nadab and Abihu began to tire
of serving outside the tabernacle door,
they filled their pans with incense and fire,
their pride left them as ashes on the floor.

When Moses had begun to swell with pride,
he struck the second stone and water flowed,
but God showed him the promised land outside,
and the anger of God hotly glowed.

When Goliath strode onto the battlefield,
the heart of all men sank and they moaned,
but his pride meant that his fate was sealed,
and a ragged shepherd boy threw his stone.

When Satan took Jesus to a high tower
and offered Him a king's ruling rod,
Satan's pride condemned Him in that hour,
when Jesus said, 'Don't test the Lord, your God.'

If this poem hasn't made it crystal clear,
then 'Pride goeth before a fall',
be humble, come before our God in fear,
and in Tiny Tim's words, 'Bless us one and all.'

Bill Hayles

Thank You Father

A paigled day
 In early May
Lush grass half-long
 To sweet mown hay
And the cuckoo mocking
 Time away

O God what glory You have given
Far beyond that for which I have striven

The virgin lust
 Of early life
Spring's laughter
 And forgotten strife
And I would pay
 In earnest thanks
For all such conditions
 In nature's ranks.

Clive Cornwall

Tidal Wave

We see it on our televisions
And don't know what to say
About the tidal wave
That happened on Boxing Day.

We see the devastation
With people losing all they had
Leaving them with memories
And a future bleak and sad.

People anxious for relatives
Not knowing whether alive or dead.
Identifying the bodies
Will be a nightmare, I've heard it said.

So we all like to help,
Doing and giving what we can.
It's hands across the sea,
Trying to work out God's plan.

Jenny Bosworth

Low Chapel Carol Service

(This poem was written after the Sunday school carol service in Low Chapel Methodist Church in Ravenstonedale, when the children took part in a 'brainstorming' session. When a question about why we celebrate Christmas was asked, the first answer was, 'When Jesus died on the Cross'.

There was excitement in the air,
A sense of wonder, hope and awe,
The children came to take their place
And bring us blessings by the score.
'Just what is Christmas all about?'
A question asked, and answers came,
'When Jesus died upon the Cross.'
'A time to sing or play a game.'

'To decorate the Christmas tree,'
'To eat some turkey, cake, mince pies,'
'To open presents gladly given
Which brings a light into our eyes.'
Then more answers one by one,
'Getting,' 'Giving,' 'Sharing,' too.
'Baby Jesus Christ was born,
He came in love for me and you.'

The lesson that we learned that day,
As children told us what they knew,
Was that Jesus Christ was born,
That is a fact we know is true;
We also know He came to die
So that our wrongs can be forgiven,
And one day we'll live with Him,
And our Father, God in Heaven.

Anne Gray

LEAVES

'What happened last night?
The temperature dropped, I caught a chill and had a terrible fright.'

'Summer's over, autumn's here,
this happens every year.'

'You're no older than me, who told you?
Did you talk to the morning dew?'

'I talked to our father, the tree,
he says this happens, this time every year you see.'

'What happens to us, we're not very old?
I know I can't take much more of this cold.'

'We set the world in colours alight,
I'm told the most magnificent sight.'

'And after we change colours, what happens then?
Do we turn back to green again?'

'Well, kind of, in away,
you could say we have another day.'

'What do you mean? You speak with a sigh,
don't tell me I have to die!'

'Autumn's winds blow hard upon us all
and to the ground each leaf shall fall.

Don't cry, in death we have rebirth,
we go back once again to Mother Earth.

In the winter we're covered with a blanket of snow,
and in the spring we nourish next year's glorious show.

It's the continuing cycle of birth, life and death,
it's enough to take away your breath.

All part of an incredible design
by the Creator, oh so fine!

Yes my brother, these are the reasons
for the Lord God's for wonderful seasons!'

Rock Peters

HIGH ALMIGHTY

Here is a Blessed Holy Lord
Jesus Christ enters our souls
Thy Holy Spirit redeem us all
Grant us we all might care with love
Reach for the highest mountain
Here is thy creator of
A beautiful world
Divine hope reigns
Console our thoughts with kindness
Ask Thy master and He will send
Give us hope with praise
Thy Lord goes with you throughout life.

Antoinette Christine Cox

EGGS AND DAFFODILS

Is 'Happy Easter' just a 'Happy Christmas'
at another time of year?
You'd almost think so with the eggs and daffodils
replacing Christmas trees and lights.
No, Easter is so much more challenging
with this outrageous claim that death is now no more,
that all the aspects of our life on Earth
which seem condemned to unfulfilment
give way to rampant joy
and the vivid sense that all our longings
unfold to be fulfilled;
that death gives way to life
and love can never die.
Easter meant bewilderment, excitement and joy
to men and women who had come to trust in Christ
until the black, dark days of helplessness
when He was betrayed and put to death
by those He came to save and liberate
from all the prisons we poor humans make
to stifle hope and crush our power to love and care.
Death seemed so final, as it always does
with those we cherish most and love;
but it has given way for Him and each of us
to love and life reborn,
and to a reassuring hope
for all the restless searchings
of our vibrant love of life.

Andrew Monaghan

PRAYER

Woke with a longing
For Your presence
Rushed out without seeing You
A busy day ahead
I reckoned so little time
To fit all in
Most was spent
Sitting in front of the box
Some spent gossiping
The rest spent staring
Into space as if nothing
Better to do
While there are tasks undone
As the day was far spent
I caught myself suddenly
Hurried through
The rest of the house chores
Yet no time to finish
Drag my tired body to bed
Remembered I didn't see You today
Quickly said a hurried prayer
Hoping You heard
With a promise of spending
More time with You tomorrow
Which never came
What a wasted day
What a wasted life
What joy if more time
Is spent seeing You
My Saviour
My day would be better
My life would be worth living

Abiodun Razak

Beliefs, Opinions And Ideas, Or Seeking Help From God

People who are full of their own beliefs, opinions and ideas
Often create much deception and fears
That are specifically designed to lead us astray
And keep us from living the proper way,
Bringing much harmony and divisions,
Causing us to make the wrong decisions,
Leading to a world of heartbreak and pain
And bringing many feelings of guilt and shame,
Also bringing much oppression and confusion,
And much spiritual darkness and disillusion.
But when we become humble enough to admit to God,
That we need His help, and cannot work things out on our own,
We can then approach His royal throne,
And when we become united in this humility,
God gives us much greater power and ability
To do things that we never thought we could do,
Because He is there to help us all the way through,
Eventually helping us to win
Over our many temptations to fall into sin.
He also gives us the ability to live in harmony with Him,
and each other,
And to love one another as sister and brother.
This is all that God needs to build a strong and united church
That will bring His love and healing to the people on the Earth.

Martin Reynolds

'To Jane - The Recollection'

(I wrote this poem for our church curate, Jane, when she left us to go and open a retreat house in Devon.)

I can't compete with Percy Bysshe,
But this is my sincerest wish -
That I may find some special way
To thank you, Jane, and then to say
How much I treasure every year
You've given in love and friendship here.
Your gracious kindness and concern
And thoughtful prayers that we may learn
To follow Christ in hope and trust,
To value all that's true and just,
To understand the sacrifice
Required of those who 'pay the price',
Committing all to His commands,
The courage that His 'call' demands;
To find the blessings He will give
To those who heed His voice, to live
A different way, and give up all,
To shine for Christ and trust His 'call';
To share His peace with all who come
For healing, prayer, for joy and fun;
To glimpse a little bit of Heaven
With Jane and Margaret down in Devon.

Nancie Cator

No Song To Sing?

Sometimes there seems no song to sing.
Time was when grocer's boy on trade bicycle
whistled so merrily within our streets.
Time was when busy mums while washing
and mangling their children's clothes,
sang beloved romantic melodies from theatre shows,
blessing our ears - delighting with its treat.
Time was too - when doting, loving parents
sang little ones to sleep to sweet cradle lullabies,
but we don't seem to do that anymore.

What happened to so many church choirs
whose Sunday songs of joy and reverence
drew us sacredly close to the Lord himself?
O England - in this vast land of choice,
what has happened to your voice?
Live we now amidst such contentious words
of rights and differences - strangling the throat
amidst multi tensions, strifes and buying things.
Does love now do without some motivating songs we really do need
to bless this diminishing existence of our souls?

O sing again - my lovelies - sing!
Let some tiny angels return again to Earth
and watch those happier babies smile.
Who knows - 'twixt divides of east and west
they could grow up to smile more often at each other,
ready to sing united choruses of love and purpose together
this time - eternally.

Don Harris

Heavenly Hieroglyphs

When there is pink in the sky, God is sending you His love,
Any time of the day, any place in your life.
A grey day with pouring rain is not a reason to be fed up or depressed
Just know that angelic window cleaners are at work.
Grey is only unpolished silver.

One of your beautiful smiles given freely to another will brighten
their day and yours too.
Aeroplane traces criss-crossing the sky is a heavenly kiss just for you.
You do not have to do anything to deserve it,
Just accept the love it is sent with.

A magnificent sunset deserves to be admired,
A heavenly artist is at work after all.

Gold or silver pathways across the sea, caused by the sun and moon,
Are the routes taken by angels when they come to visit.

Finally when you take the time to see the pictures in the clouds,
Then you will have opened your God mail.
He sends it every day.

Dolly Little

THE CROSS OF CHRIST

The brave men in the trenches,
They too shared in the cross of Christ,
Infested with lice and rats,
Up to their necks in mud
At Passchendaele, they longed to go home.
It was stalemate for four years.
The young German, dying,
Shot through the breast, was
In a British rear line hospital.
A young English nurse, a woman,
Held his head in her hands,
To comfort him in his dying agony.
'I want to go home to my farm
On the Rhine,' he gasped, and passed away.
The young nurse wept bitterly -
They both shared in the cross of Christ.

R O'Shaughnessy

VAPORISED COUNTENANCE

When I pass you in Heaven and have nothing left to say
There will be an air of a new stand of vaporised countenance
With another pour and theft to your old way

There will be another order of carrying out tasks which we perform
Where its skill has a border which is purer,
Higher and separates us from the norm

Where white foundations in Heaven will become as pillars of stability,
With right roundations in his some of righteous forfillity.

With the same attitude as Joshua when the city walls came tumbling,
A gratitude of wit and calls crumbling.

Another Nevil Halls lining another patient set up,
Another evil defining and met of his cup.

Fiona Clarke

ANDREW

A is for the angels up in Heaven.
N is for Nazareth, a market town in Galilee.
D is for the darkness of the world.
R is for the repentance of your sins.
E is for eternal life of God.
W is for the water being turned into wine.

Join these letters together and you will get one of the apostles,
The brother of Simon called Peter.
And Jesus said, if you follow me, I will make you a fisher of men.

Nancy Elliott

THE FOUR QUESTIONS

I had a dream, I was standing in front of the good Lord,
There to be judged.
There is a silence, five, ten, twenty seconds go by,
Finally the good Lord speaks,
'You are John, what have you to say for yourself John.'
'I was not without sin, Lord.'
'So John, tell me something new, only one man went through
Your world who was without sin, He was my son.'
'Yes Lord, I know.'
'No John you do not know. So John what else do you have to say.'
'Well Lord I spoke with Solomon on the way to see You Lord,
I hope You don't mind.'
'No John I don't mind. Solomon in all his wisdom couldn't answer
Your four questions could he?'
'No Lord.'
'Well John I hold up my hands in surrender, I too cannot answer
Your four questions, come in.'

John Morrison

A Certain Kind Of Beauty

Creation, a flower blooming in the golden sunlight,
A traveller resting by silent streams,
Secret whispers of love, two hearts joined in marriage,
A swallow flying over high seas,
The rolling waves, a crimson horizon,
White doves over sandy beaches,
The voice of unity where equality flourishes,
A peaceful nation,
Yet none are like a sweet Messiah who died for me.

Gill Thomas

God's Rosebuds

My mother had a decent voice,
Who sang the favourites of her choice.
And in the past she proved to me
That only God could make a tree.
Now with the years of stress and strain
And evil deeds for greed and gain,
I wonder sometimes if my faith
Is weakening like a fading wraith.
Then came this morning wonderfully
A neighbour with a gift for me.
Two perfect rosebuds in her hand
How could I fail to understand?
So now my faith is much restored
Belief in Him is more assured
I know in poetry or prose
That only God could make a rose.

Margaret Thorpe

TOTAL FORGIVENESS

Total forgiveness is what we have in our Lord Jesus Christ,
Many people especially ladies say I don't need forgiveness, I am nice.
Because I am not a sinner; a lot of charity works I do every day,
I am sure to go to Heaven when I die is what they do say.
Alas we are all sinners from head to toe in God's sight,
We all do wrong then say that it is a white lie, it's alright.
We can all convince ourselves but God is not fooled at all,
We will all answer for what we've done at the last bugle call.
Then those who are relying on good works will soon realise,
They were pointless for they cannot get in Heaven now they have died.
Only those who have accepted Jesus as their saviour will enter in,
It is not down to any good works they have done but Jesus took away their sin.
I was fortunate, I knew very well I was a sinner, perhaps the worst there has been,
But I met with Jesus and His love, then He did wash me totally clean,
In His precious blood that He shed on that cross at Calvary,
There He suffered and died to set this sinner totally free.
If you still claim you're not a sinner and will get into Heaven by good works alone,
You are in for a mighty shock because all the good works you've done will not atone,
For the sins that hang like chains that you drag around everywhere,
Won't you accept Jesus Christ as your own saviour and be of good cheer.
Then I am sure in Heaven one day we will meet,
And praise our Saviour while sitting at His feet.

Don Goodwin

LIFE'S JOURNEY

Asphalt roads of discovery
Lead to the junction of consciousness
As the sun sets on youth
With the pendulum of life
Swinging profusely towards death
One remembers time felt precious things
Homilies to the forsaken
Litanies to the abandoned of war and love
As the town clock strikes atonement
From promises not kept - sins not forgiven
One reflects on the immortality of the soul
Within the incandescence of a mature troubled mind
And wonders what lies beyond the grave
In the intermittent clutches of fleeting despair
At the fragility and transience of life.

Finnan Boyle

The Birth Of Jesus

It was our Father up above
Who sent His child out of love
Baby Jesus is His name

To Mount Calvary He has came
To His death He would go
With all His bravery He would show

He died for us upon that cross
To the Christians it's a loss
In chapel we call His name
And thank Him for our greatest gain

Mary and Joseph His mum and dad
To lose their son it must be sad

Christmas comes but once a year
So give that child a great big cheer

John Arthur Williams

Bedtime Poem

Thank You for the rising sun
And the morsel today that I can rely on
Thank You for my family and friends
You gave as if lending new ears
Thank You for my life God

God I am throwing my burdens on You
For You promise to make my many aches few
Sorry for anything I forget
My aching knees are thanking You for the sunset

Angela Nevo Hopkins

GREYHOUNDS R US

God sent His angels down to Earth,
To search for teachers true.
They came and were disheartened,
Until they found a few,
They brought us all together,
A rescue we became,
Saving all the greyhounds,
Now, what about a name?
We played around with titles,
I suppose that's what one does.
With spiritual intervention,
God said, '*Greyhounds R Us*'.

Pat Senior

WEEDS

Isn't it strange how the weeds seem to grow?
A shower of rain and before you know,
The flowers are shaded by weeds tall and strong,
Revealing themselves where they just don't belong.
You carefully get down on bended knee,
Removing the weeds so the flowers can see.
Then two days later, who knows why?
They're all there again in the blink of an eye.
This reminds me of sin and the way that it works,
Weedling in, to reach where it hurts.
Entering the lives of people each day,
Ruining the things that they do and they say.
Turning what's good into something so bad,
Making the lives of people so sad.
If we open our eyes we'll plainly see,
That now is the time for bended knee,
To say sorry Lord for the wrong we've done -
And thank You Lord for sending Your son.
The weeds in our lives will never take hold,
Forgiveness is ours through our saviour we're told.

Jeanne Rouse

My Prayer

Grant me, I pray
Each and every day
Strength to embrace
And face
Whatever is to be,
Lord, I ask of Thee
Be Thou near

Be my friend
Until life's end
Share my troubles
Ease my fear
Lord, I ask of Thee
Be Thou near

Lord be in my happiness
Share my joy
Be my light
In the darkness of the night
Take my hand
Help me to understand
Lead me

Lord, I ask of Thee
Be Thou near.

Emma Hood

THY REWARD IN HEAVEN

Faith lifts the veil before our eyes, beyond
The withering blasts of time; the sweeter heavens

Balm to heal the deeper wound our spirits feel,
Beneath the rod that's sent in love, nor droop

In sadness or in fear where verdant fields in
Beauty rise, then let us hope, 'tis not in vain

The harvest brings the blissful moment near,
For Thy reward awaits above, through moistened

By our grief the soil, for they shall reap who
Sow in tears, when we in glory shall appear,

Toil, on a little longer here, rich gladness through eternal years,
Beneath the rod that's sent in love.

Imogene Lindo

BLOOD

Life is in the blood
flowing within.
Life-blood is food, and nourishment
and strength.
Every creature's essence.
Our shared heritage.
Yet, everywhere
it ebbs away, prematurely, wickedly,
into the earth,
staining the places
where we try to live.
Bad blood is synonymous
with sin and evil . . .
How shall it be cleansed?
God, in His wisdom,
chose the innocent blood,
of the one He calls 'Son'
to be offered freely
in expiation
of all that is evil.
Thus it becomes
the great sign, symbol and conveyance
of His love and redemption
for all humanity.
With reverence then,
we give thanks,
as we break bread, and sip wine,
together.

Jo Allen

INNER CITY PRAYER

Tonight I shall not fear
nor dread the coming of dark
stars into my orbit

for He is with me and bright
is the corona of His vision
in the fastness of the night

this night I will sleep within Him
within the hollow of His breast
enclosed in His protection and His love

His heart shall beat within me
within me and for me
and His breath will bless me

may His blessings be upon the shooters
slumped insensible in filthy alleys and byways
may their dope be cut safely and their syringes clean

may His blessings be upon the weeping drunks
who gash their wrists on their smashed windows
may they learn peace and the strength to love themselves

may His blessings be upon the women who loiter
let the kerb crawlers respect them
may they be merciful and leave pitiful lives unbroken

may His blessings be upon the wretched
homeless in their cardboard hovels
may they be saved from drinking meths so they can sleep

may He bless all those who drift in confusion
mumbling to themselves or ranting unheeded by the uncaring
may they come at last to Him and find peace

in a world too self-indulgent to care
may He bless all these broken people
may He send the balm of angels among them.

Hamish Lee

Look All Around You

Look all around you, what do you see?
The work of God is all around thee
Blue sky above, earth at your feet
Just look all around you it's such a treat
He gave us the grass, He gave us the trees
All of these things He gave us to please
He gave us the clouds, He gave us the sea
Most of all He gave us you and me
Look further in the beauty you will see
Don't just glance it will escape thee
Each flower petal that opens
Every bird that sings a song
Every piece of nature God never got it wrong
Beauty everywhere makes us feel good each day
When we look around and see God provided it this way.

Margaret Ward

WHO IS GOD?

So who or what is God to you
What makes your darkness light
You say He's kind
You say He's good
You say He puts things right

You say He speaks - but do you hear
What He says to you
Is He loud
Is He soft
Can I hear Him too

Can you see Him - are you sure
You really know He's there
Is He black
Is He white
Is He everywhere

When you're hurting - does He know
Can He ease the pain
If you weep
Does He come
To dry your tears again

I too have often pondered
Questions such as these
We each have
Our perception
Of who or what God is

Judith MacBeth

Chapel Of Peace

When you feel lonely and there's no one to care
Go to the chapel He's waiting there
Go to the chapel, the chapel of peace
Where every whisper is listened to, every whisper you speak
Go to the chapel He understands
He's right there beside you, just reach out your hands
When you have loved someone, heart, body and soul
You've lost them, they're gone and you're out of control
Go to Him He's waiting and your pain will cease
You will find comfort where silence is peace
You can share all your trouble, all your hurt and your fear
He is a friend there to listen, each word He will hear
So go to Him He's waiting and He understands
He's right there beside you, just reach out your hands
Just reach out your hands.

Beryl Barlow

Spare A Dime

Christmas time's a special time
And one that 'we' should share
When you hear the words 'spare a dime'
Just show 'them' that you care.

The fairy sits upon the tree
She has her magic wand,
A symbolic angel is what I see
It fills my heart with song.

And Jesus born to me and you
To fill 'our' children with laughter
A special gift from God, it's true
With love forever after.

Some are not so lucky
Not like 'you' or 'I'.
Take care that you should think of others
And make them smile not cry.

For Christmas time is special
A time when we should care
There's an abundance of love within our hearts,
It's a time for us to share.

April Dickinson-Owen

Salute To A Saviour

They crucified Him on the Calvary Cross,
The world's most saddest loss.
What did He do to warrant that pain,
He loves mankind,
His devotion doesn't wane.
It happened because they didn't understand,
The truth and kindness
Of this Son of Man.

But we know He remains with us,
Through winter snow and summer dust.
The friend you talk to in times of strife,
And He'll give us eternal life
With His Father in holy paradise.
No more condemnation,
No more lies.

The tears that raked down His face,
Each droplet helped save
The human race.
An awful crown of thorns
Thrust upon His head.
They thought they could destroy Him,
But He's not dead.

He's with us every waking hour,
The light of goodness
Shines from an ivory tower.
So let's get on our knees,
Pay homage to Him,
The only one that
Can save us from mortal sin.

Gary Monaghan

Cradle To The Grave

Loveable
Innocent
Fearless
Erudite

Leisure
Independence
Families
Emotions

Lament
Impasse
Foreseeable
Eternal

D Atkinson

A Question

When Jesus washed disciples' feet,
What was it meant to show?
That we should serve our neighbours not
Exchanging blow for blow?
Or could it be to demonstrate
God's love for all below?

Peter Spurgin

Where Were You God?

Where were You God on that fateful day
When so many lives were taken away?
Lives of little children burnt or killed by a gun,
For nothing at all could they have possibly done.
Even tiny tots who could just about stand
Too innocent to try to understand
Why they and the adults who suffered the same fate
Were killed by fanatics so full of hate.

Our hearts go out to those in sorrow
To those people of Beslan who can see no tomorrow.
So many families are now torn apart,
Homes full of grief and broken hearts.
Those young survivors, will they ever forget,
I very much doubt it, I say with regret.
So where were You God on that fateful day
When those innocent lives were blasted away?

Phyllis Ing

The Dawn

When I arose at early morn
And viewed the garden in the dawn,
Festooned across the greenery,
Was a spider spun catenary.
Constructed in the black of night
Now visible in the morning light.
It glistened in an early dew
Bejewelled with a brilliant hue.
Reflected by a source of light
That bade farewell unto the night.
The hand of *God* is never still
As nature heeds the creator's will.

Bill Austin

On The Imitation Of Christ

A handsome herring gull
  stood white on a rooftop in the morning sun,
  looking very large and still . . .
I also was having a break,
  but I had a cup of tea . . .
  Was the gull looking at me?
  Perhaps the bird could see
  my streptocarpus or cape primrose
  at my window sill . . .
Perhaps the gull did take
  the white flowers there
  for baby birds.
My father once asked, 'Do animals think?'
  We can surely suppose
  dogs and cats and horses do;
  eagles pre-calculate'
  budgies and parrots use words . . .
Whereas - with humans
  the subconscious mind
  (in expanding God-ward)
  is infinitely understanding
  with no limit in
  imitating our Lord
  till we find Him
  within.

V Irvine-Fortescue

THE DARK MAN

In the shadows stands a man
Whose face I cannot see
A misty image - hidden,
I wonder who he could be.

He skulks in the darkest corners,
In the recesses of my mind.
Burrowing ever deeper
To see what he might find.

All of my insecurities
He is determined he should know.
So I have to close that door
And be careful what I show.

When I hear those honeyed tones
Dripping with soothing balm,
I give myself a shake,
To wake up my internal alarm,

Or before too long I'll slip
Into the quicksand of his words,
Disappearing in to another realm
His voice - the last I heard.

Standing in the shadows, he waits,
But I'll not be his prey.
For I've come back from the brink,
I live to fight another day.

Beware you weary travellers,
He's not what he may seem.
He lives in our waking world
Not in the land of dream.

Christina Andrea

'When I Say 'I Am In Pain' I Am At Any Rate Justified Before Myself' Wittgenstein

At least another could see me unable to get off the floor.

Trawl religion for pain
Massive in the prophets
Wasteland
The pain of apostasy
Buddha.
Calls for Anatta
Under Vatican walls,
Fitting to talk of
'Non-self'.
Somehow all religions
Imply pain.
Zoroaster
The great untruth
Lies,
Al Hallaj
Sufi
To you
My thoughts turn
On Good Friday.

My problem
The grit and real
Empirical determinism.
Like meeting a madman
There is
No rational answer
To pain.
My cousin
Veteran of Dunkirk and India
Deeply hurt me mocking religion.
'Trust the doctors,' he said.
Three weeks later he was dead . . .

Paul Faulkner

TEARS OF THE HEART!

Tears of angels or near, at the death of a child

Tears of the heart, is when the letter comes in to men's hands
Saying, 'Your son or daughter has died in war.'

Tears of the heart or many. From the time of birth till death,
It is an enthusiastic minefield of tears and laughter.

Tears of the heart can be many,
From the death of a loved one, to the birth of a loved one.

Tears of the heart can be many, from the day we marry,
Till we part ways.

Tears of the heart can be word spoken,
That we will be regretting later.

Tears of the heart can be when we see our Lord,
On our homecoming to His presents.

Tears come when my Lord says,
'Welcome home my child!'

James Allan Jorgensen

EVENING RECITAL

Lord please help some poor soul today
And all of those who have gone astray
Especially those with a broken heart
Dear Lord, dear Lord forgive.

Lord if I have said words to offend
Lord please forgive and give love to lend
Should I give thought or have to send
Please Lord, yes Lord forgive.

Forgive my sins I confess this night
And all those secrets of Your mighty fight
Guide me safely to Your distant light
Dear Lord, dear Lord forgive.

If I have uttered idle words in vain
If I have turned aside for want or gain
Lest I offend thru stress or strain
Dear Lord, dear Lord forgive.

If I have used others on my way
Lord let me help those who have gone astray
Guide me, love me and my saviour be
Dear Lord, dear Lord forgive.

Ray Duncan

Calm Before The Storm

Christmas is a time for thanksgiving, rejoicing and praise
Treats for the family, halcyon days
Times of idyllic holidays in far away lands
Cocktails and palm trees, azure seas and white silky sands.

People unwinding, enjoying their break
Then a tsunami hit, bringing loss and heartache
Homes are brutally smashed, families forlorn
Death struck relentless, elderly, young, some barely been born.

We gaze at their faces, share in their stress
Donate some of our money, but it does not make that pain less
Orphans and widows, total families lost
The damage is endless, too vast to cost.

Across every nation, whatever the divide
We stand shattered, yet united, cultures put aside
Nature has sent a blow from the sea
Shooting a warning both to you and me
But despite the hurt that's been caused when the debris did spew
Kindness and love had the strength to shine through.

Kay Fordham

I'LL BE SAFE

When you're shining down from afar
My brightest shining, wishing star
I know we will be safe.

I'll think of you every day
Everyone's got thoughts in different ways
I remember a tear when we said goodbye
But now it's us that's left to cry.

A strong person who remains in my heart
Remains our happiness which will never part
Dad, Grandad there from the start
With loads of love and a tender heart.

A thought of you may bring a tear of sadness
But maybe regret
Tears of joy and also upset
But a memory of strength that can always be kept.

Remembering times in younger days
Sly and secret little ways
To put a smile on your face
At that time and place.

Now as we get older we realise
There's more to life beyond our eyes
There's a heart that's made of pure gold
From when you were young to now you are old
But a treasure to remain true
Dad, Grandad our thoughts, our memories of you
Because make us proud you always do.

Sadness that you've been took away
But kept in our hearts to always stay.
But happiness as you were and still are
A part of us in our soul.

You gave us our strength
You were strong
In our hearts now you belong.

Michelle Barnes

EACH LITTLE SOUL

Everything comes to he who waits,
This is the story I'm told,
Tell that to the boy with the big sad brown eyes,
Just a few grains of rice in his bowl.

Tell that to the baby who cries all alone,
In a war ravaged country, so cold,
Tell that to a mum with a babe at her breast,
Whose life milk no longer flows.

Tell that to the young girl in nightmare's hell,
As into slavery she's sold,
To abuse unthinkable, her innocence gone,
Relieved only when death takes its toll.

Tell the millions of babies starving each day,
They never will live to grow old,
I pray that the rich man will think with his heart,
And surrender a portion of gold.

Tells in the Bible, not one sparrow dies,
Without our God knows of its fall,
Tells of a Heaven where all children smile,
Pure paradise for each little soul.

Everything comes to he who waits,
This is the story I'm told,
Dear Lord take the hurting, the babies their tears,
In your safe arms of love, please enfold.

Dorothy M Mitchell

THE LAST LAUGH

One day I sat upon a train,
It was cold and grey, with spits of rain.
I had a seat though many stood
And hung on straps as best they could.
The windows closed against the chill,
As early March was wintry still.

A smell curled up into my nose;
A smell so foul my senses froze.
Other nostrils twitched and flared;
No one spoke as no one dared.
With lowered lids I glanced around,
But source of stench could not be found.

I asked myself what it might be.
There was no reason I could see.
Sweaty sneakers? Unwashed feet?
Something dead below the seat?
It's awful how some folks don't wash,
Though all dressed up and looking posh.

We thundered on along the line;
At least we would arrive on time.
In Lisbon I got off the train,
Relieved, I breathed fresh air again.
And then I saw what caused the pooh;
A lump of dog's muck on *my shoe*!

The moral here is clear to see,
It's not always 'them', sometimes it's me!

Jenny Fernandes

TSUNAMI '04

Boxing Day 26th past December,
just after family joy remember.
But this was another day
tsunami; Indian Ocean way.

Beneath tranquil dark blue,
mankind on Earth no clue.
For our wonderful Earth,
this day brought death!

Eden's paradise palms blow,
sand and warm waves flow.
Did God punish mankind?
Within Heaven, anger find.

Now terror, people run,
tourist place, exotic fun,
huge waves crashed coast near,
like satanic stranger to fear!

Many souls washed away,
loved with names; pray.
Now coastland silent waste,
unknown souls buried; haste.

Women and men gone!
Boys and girls gone!
Old and young not spared,
worldwide shock and shared.

The faiths of people wonder,
Devil maybe, God's act ponder.
Like Bible Noah's world flood truth,
cruel fate taken, lost life's breath!

Water gives life,
water takes life.
Equal measures, bad and good,
mortal, fragile, understood.

Three minutes reflection, silence,
ask God why souls lost existence?
Remember hope seventh day, (Rev: 20)
God's Heaven promise say . . .

George Woodford

The Whisper Of God

Enfolded within the petal of the rose
Is Mary's tear
The snowdrop, the purity of her love
Blossoms every year

In the stillness of the night
Shadows and moonlight
Comes to the ear
Whispers from God
Ever near

He is in the gentle rain
Gale force winds the trees bend low
The cross of pain, and yet we know
The whisper of God is our saving Grace
His breath against our face

Whisper of God Thou speaks to me
In the sighing of the breeze
The warmth of the sun Thy breath
My soul at ease

The glory of the world, night and day
Come what may, we can hear
The whisper of God, know His Grace
Feel His breath against our face.

Emma Hood

STARLIGHT

Trudging through the sleety lamplight,
Eyes fixed firmly
On frost bound earth.
Look up! Look up!
And view above
Breath-snatching awe of the star filled night.

You will not see a red sleigh climb,
Or hear the reindeers' harness bells.
No angels fill the celestial sphere,
No supernova flares in time.
Instead we watch the galaxies
Composing music so sublime.

These age-old witnesses of life,
Whose light shone on
The birth of Christ,
Look down and see
Our 'Winterfest'
And wonder at our modern hype.

The gorging, presents, 'Follow the trend',
Have we really lost the plot?
Is the nucleus of His message
Rooted deep to be called forth?
When my desperate 'Neighbour' calls me,
Will I answer, 'Yes, my friend,
We will strive to keep this planet
Dancing to its *natural* end.'

Meg Fraser

A Psalm Of Generation X

(Based on Psalm 91)

The Lord is my nuclear bunker
I shall not be afraid
He is my gas mask and my tank
What can man do to me?

He is the bedrock of my soul
I shall not be shaken

A thousand may fall at my side
Ten thousand at my right hand
But the Lord will keep me from all harm
My trust is in Him

The angel of the Lord camps around
Those who respect the Lord
Who love Him with their whole hearts

Do not put your trust in money
Or the power of a bomb
Put your faith in Yahweh, the Lord of Hosts
He is God Almighty;
Might to save

Put your trust in Jesus Christ
He is Adonai and El Shaddai
His blood has broken the power of death.

Ruth Ellett

Above The Tower

(The tower being the Tower Colliery)

I pulled off the road and stopped the car,
then stood on that mountain high.
The frost in the air took my breath away,
as I shivered beneath my coat.

But it mattered not that my fingers froze,
and the tip of my nose turned red,
for I'll never forget the magical sight
that spread before my eyes.

The valley in darkness, with twinkling lights
like fairyland far below,
and on the horizon, the snow covered hills
rose up through the pale pink haze.

An eerie light spread over the sky
as the evening turned to night,
and the air was still, as I stood in awe
of the beauty I can't describe.

Perhaps never again would it look like this,
but God let me glimpse, just once,
and now it is etched upon my heart,
remembered till the end of time.

Maureen Powell

A Quiet Moment

Will you spare a quiet moment
To speak to God in prayer?
Tell Him that you'll listen
Tell Him that you care.

You don't need fancy words
Speak to Him as a friend.
God will always listen
On that you can depend.

Tell Him about the people
That have crossed your path today.
Tell Him how you were feeling
As you went along your way.

Tell Him what makes you happy,
Tell Him what makes you blue.
Involve Him in your life
In everything you do.

Share your life with God
And He'll share His love with you.
He'll always be there for you
No matter what you do.

His love is really precious
Don't throw it all away.
Just spare a quiet moment
And speak to God today.

Christine Collins

COURAGE

Give me courage, Lord, I ask,
To face ahead this daunting task.
To walk with you, through every day,
My difficult and tiring way.

Make my thoughts more positive,
Give my heart the will to live.
Be in my mind and share my pain,
Please make my body whole again.

Take my hand and lead me past
This suffering, which will not last,
To a better place in time,
Where peace of mind once more is mine.

Be my friend, my loyal guide.
Listen to my prayers, abide
Within me every day.
Please God, take my fear away.

Lorna Lea

From My Heart

From my heart I thank You, *Lord*, for each bright new day,
I thank You too for 'being there' as I amble on my way.
I know You're there beside me, I feel Your presence - strong,
Your peace that reigns within my soul is with me all day long.

When times of earthly troubles have plagued me one by one,
You've lifted up my spirit 'til all the fear is gone.
I know You test me constantly, to see if I can cope,
I hope I do You justice, *Lord*, I really do - I hope!

To feel Your peace is wonderful, I simply opened up my heart,
I asked that You'd forgive me - if I did my 'earthly' part,
I said I would not fight You if You deemed my time had come,
I would surrender without question if my time on Earth was done.

You gave me strength to carry on through troubled waters deep,
I know You're there beside me - even when I sleep.
I feel Your love supporting me through times of deep despair,
I shrug my shoulders with a smile - I know that You are there.

I see You in the morning dew upon the grass so green,
On flower petals large and small - in ponds where water gleams.
I feel You in each breath I take, each thought that fills my mind,
I know You're part of all I do, gentle, loving, kind.

My wish is that I serve You, *Lord*, in all things that I do,
To offer up some gratitude - and sing in praise of You.
I know I'll fail You sometimes - and Your forgiveness I will seek,
This I know for sure, *Lord*, cos I'm human - and I'm weak.

And when my time on Earth is done and You call out my name,
My wish is that You'll take me 'home', from whence I feel I came.
To spend eternity with You - in Heaven - close by Your side,
And grant that I may know Your peace in the house where You reside.

Gloria Courts

JESUS

When you walk with Jesus, you walk with love,
When you talk with Jesus, you talk with the Lord,
If you pray with Jesus, you pray with God,
And if you listen to God, you listen to the Lord.

If you live for Jesus, you live for the Lord,
If you die for Jesus, you die for God,
If you give for Jesus, you receive God's love,
You are never without from above.

When you look for Jesus, you look for the light,
If you find the light, you have found the Lord.
If you do these things for the Father above,
You'll receive these gifts from Jesus with love.

George Terry

EARTH

God's green landscape never fails to surprise,
His tiny insects, His butterflies,
Each one perfect in every way,
Busy each surviving a brand new day.

Worms wriggling through the soil,
Ants, slugs and snails who busily toil,
Beetles and ladybirds, hoverflies, dragonflies - spiders too,
Spinning their webs in the morning dew.

Clouds drifting slowly across the blue sky,
Making patterns in my mind's eye,
Sun's rays warming the damp brown earth
Ready for the rich soil to give birth
To the flowers that will brighten even the darkest of days,
And they will appear in plenty during the month of May.

Everything has its place here on Earth,
Enjoy it while we can - spring's the time of rebirth.

Christine Hardemon

God's Promise In The Rainbow

See a rainbow arch in a rainswept sky,
Seven colours glisten in the sun's rays,
Red and orange like fire's flames leaping high,
Join with yellow, green, like sun on a bay.
Blue, indigo, violet - royal shades,
Complete the bow the Master set above,
When plucking Noah from a watery grave,
He made this promise showing His great love.
Harvest, in its turn, would follow spring birth,
Seasons would eternally come and go,
Never again would floods devastate Earth,
This the Lord God's message of the rainbow.
When I see His coloured arc flash above,
I'm assured of His promise and true love!

Pat Heppel

Those Other Things

(St John 21. 25. And there are many other things which Jesus did, the which, if they should be written every one, I suppose that even the world itself could not contain the books that should be written)

Thanks Lord, for these other things.
Imagination often yields up truth.
We know You taught upon the mountainside.
Perhaps one night there came a girl called Ruth,
whose long sealed eyes You caused to open wide.

(Thanks Lord for these other things.)
The next day You found her where lilies grew
and Ruth was grateful when You stopped and said
one bloom was pink, the others white and blue.
For scents she'd known, must now to colours wed.

Thanks Lord, for these other things.
Compassion like warmth in Your smiling face.
Anger like ice for those inflicting pain.
We know You better by this other grace.
These things may surely make Your will more plain.

Thanks Lord, for these other things.
They give us scope to know how You will be
when dealing with the problems of the day,
helping us to walk with you fearlessly.
Trusting that in all things You are the way.

M Munro Gibson

THE DAILY ROUND - SUNSET AND SUNRISE

Now goes the light
And comes the night;
Oh, what a sight
That ends the day.

It brings to mind
That God is kind
And how we find
He's there always.

Then comes the dawn
That brings the morn.
Once more is born
A brand new day.

It brings us hope
That we will cope
And not just grope
Along life's way.

So hear my prayer -
Let sun prepare
To leave its lair,
It's hideaway,

And shine its rays
To shed malaise -
Dispelling haze -
Throughout the day.

David Varley

TREES

In spring the trees reach into Heaven,
Their green leaves leap into the sky,
In summer they are gentle friends,
That seem to smile as the winds sigh.
In autumn they turn every park
Into a golden mystery,
But winter is their time for prayer,
In silver, snowy worlds a tree
Becomes an artist's dream to paint,
As it stands lowly in the sod,
Our hearts like poets see the trees,
Arrows that point the way to God.

Marion Schoeberlein

I'M YOUR FOREVER FRIEND

Do not worry and don't despair
For I am with you, I'm always there
When you're in pain and suffering too
I'm always there, I am with you
Your thoughts, your feelings, please with me share
For I am with you, I'm always there
So do not worry and don't despair
Carry everything always, to me in prayer
My name is Jesus, forever I'll love you
I'm your forever friend, forever be mine too
What peace you'll often forfeit, what needless pain you'll bare
If to me you do not carry, everything each time in prayer.

Royston Davies

The Fire

The fire is burning
it burns within my soul
it burns everywhere
words within me speak

flocks have gone astray
out there on their own
no shepherd leads the way
they have lost their way

once they caught the word
they had a life
they brightened the place
darkness left their lives

they went through the door
the light showed the way
the salt seasoned the taste
and the devil had no place

many have taken the wine
they lay drunk on streets
darkness fills everywhere
the city lay in waste

there in my soul
the fire I cannot stay
how I feel to speak
there is no time for me

Now comes a new shepherd
words of a new heaven
no one meet the devil
usher in a new earth.

Frank Xora

PRESENCE

The old terror holds him, her, no more.
Grief just spoken, joy just spoken;
quenching cries of a thirst only you can satisfy,
eyes wide open in wonder
for the wonder of alleluia.
A prayer is still echoing your final cry:
'Forgive us, for we know not
what we do, failing to surrender to you.'
To share your father's infinite mercy,
freedom and power,
you are our flesh, food,
our good elder brother,
eternal instant of our 'yes'
to your kingdom of love.

Angela Matheson

Our Split In Life

We want the world to know there is many in me
All of us desire to be safe, warm and free

We have seen many things, with these precious eyes
And for what we have seen, we have had to tell many lies

We split off one at a time is true
For the torture was too great for one to go through

The pain, suffering torture left us in great misery
One day someone asked Jesus' help and He heard our plea

One by one we each asked God's son in our heart
And with that Jesus gives us a brand new start

As we each accepted Jesus it became plain to see
What life that we were living, was not what it should be

Instead of pain, fear and great aftermath
Jesus offered us peace, love and hope if we followed *His* path

So now as we prepare for journey of freedom, safety and to heal
Many are tired, battered and scared or not sure how to feel

We are trusting in Jesus, God's only begotten son
Who has our path mapped and guides for this day to come

For in *His* will we desire to be
And with Him and many others we will be set *free*

Anclise Monique

CRUCIFIXION

Are you aware, have you a clue?
Jesus died on the cross for you.
He died on that cross for all mankind,
His mother wept, but it had been defined.
Piercing His head was a crown of thorns,
He was crucified in the early dawn.
Darkness fell all around,
On that sad Calvary mound.
One day He'll walk this Earth again,
For that is what the scriptures ordain.

Zoiyar Cole

ALWAYS THERE FOR ME

Thanks for Your help today dear Lord
without You what would I do.
Always there when I need someone
my troubles to guide me through.

No matter how small the job may be
I know I am not alone
when trying any task to solve
You will help me get it done.

So please accept my gratitude
in problems great and small
which I never tackle on my own
You are always there when I call.

So thanks for Your help today dear Lord
for I knew the task I could do
as I gathered my tools together
my prayer was reaching You.

Ruth Barclay Brook

GOD'S HIDDEN TREASURE

I've discovered something new,
A glimmer of the real me.
Like a buried treasure covered in grime
As the dirt is wiped away;
There is a glimpse of me,
The diamond that lies beneath is beginning to shine.
Just a small crack to start,
Like the morning sun peeping through the curtains.
You see, I have been hidden for so long,
All that was visible was the layers of dirt, accumulated over the years.
All the hurt, the pain from life's trials,
They have all left a scar.
But God is cleaning me up, stripping back the layers.
And through all that muck I can just about see
A small hole, a crevice in which I lie beneath.
As a diamond glistens in the sun, reflecting the light,
So beautiful God has made me.
As God shines His light upon me,
I like what I see.
Sometimes it hurts to get cleaned up,
There are many layers and stains.
The paint stripper stings as it seeps into my wounds.
But God has a gentle touch and He wipes away my tears.
Though I wriggle and squirm in His revealing light,
God doesn't give up, for He knows what lies beneath.
He keeps rubbing away, peeling back the layers,
And slowly the crack begins to widen.
God puts in His hand and pulls me out,
The grime has been cleaned away.
And here I am glistening before His eyes,
God's beautiful hidden treasure.

A Millward

DIALOGUE WITH GOD

When I think, I grieve
how God has turned me, now;
though I always try
to His laws bow.

Or is it my destiny
in being so,
I always tried
as far as I know.

Though I am not
one of the few,
I always tried
to abide with You.

On second thought
it is not my fault,
You made me so
why give me tort.

Lost all my battles
retreated in despair,
trying to find You
but, You were not there.

Francis Xavier Farrugia

INFORMATION

We hope you have enjoyed reading this book - and that you will continue to enjoy it in the coming years.

If you like reading and writing poetry drop us a line, or give us a call, and we'll send you a free information pack.

Alternatively if you would like to order further copies of this book or any of our other titles, then please give us a call or log onto our website at www.forwardpress.co.uk

Triumph House Information
Remus House
Coltsfoot Drive
Peterborough
PE2 9JX
(01733) 898102